CHECKING OUT

TIM PEELER

CHECKING OUT

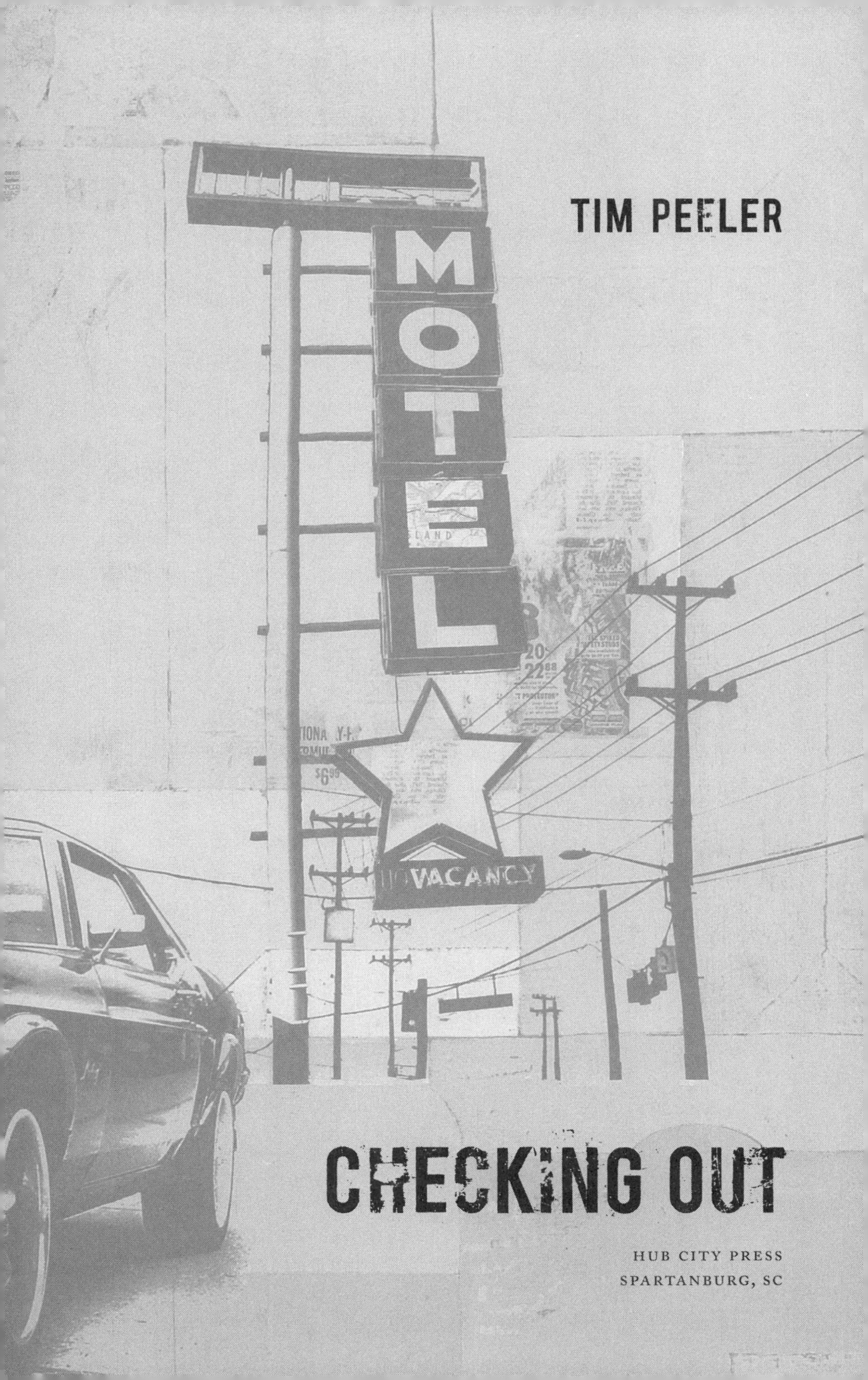

HUB CITY PRESS
SPARTANBURG, SC

Library of Congress
Cataloging-in-Publication Data

Peeler, Tim, 1957–
Checking Out / Tim Peeler.
p. cm.
ISBN 978-1-891885-71-6
1. Title.
PS3566.E276C47 2010
811'.54—dc22
2009043009

First printing, February 2010

Book design: Emily Smith
Cover: "Desert Star Motel"
© Robert Mars
Section dividers: detail from artwork
© Robert Mars

Hub City Press
149 S. Daniel Morgan Avenue
Suite 2
Spartanburg, SC 29306
864.577.9349 · 864.577.0188
www.hubcity.org

With Gratitude and in Explanation

For their feedback on these poems and enduring support, I wish to thank Gary Mitchem, David Dickson, Ron Rash, and Carter Monroe.

Thanks as always to Penny, Aaron, and Thomas who have shared not only the tough times but many good ones as well.

Much appreciation and respect for the ongoing work of Betsy Teter, John Lane, and the good folks at Hub City.

A word of explanation is in order for the "Prelude" to these poems. It is in fact a nod to seventy-five years of the Peeler family lore, both real and imagined. Decades later, the poem does, however, draw heavily on the latter.

Finally, I must offer my gratitude to the Lail and Mull families for making me for a time a part of their vibrant, successful hotel businesses. No writer could have asked for a more fertile training ground. Nor could one be more thankful for the harvest.

This one is for the hotel guys: Frank Murphy, Lawrence Heafner, Johnny Bolick, Bobby Hare, and Cooke Mull.

Contents

Prelude

Along the spina bifida backbone creek,
rotten dandelions, cow pies, tufts of thistle,
on the huge oak stump, the barefoot child,
shirtless in overalls stands, pulpit invisible.
The congregation of chickens pecks corn
he's scattered, heads jerking to earth, back,
red beards quivering as the child recites
the 23rd Psalm, and the sun elevators through
the maples beyond the meadow
where he's seen angels.

The roof has many angles:
hilltop, two story, 30's brick,
ivy running the wall behind the den.
A crew cut boy stands on either side
of what is powerfully big to him,
tossing a worn baseball over the peak:
gravity, pace, spin, physics, luck, and
magic determine which plane
the brown leather sphere will take—
the game, to make the catch without lying.

The red headed boy wanders
through the woods at grandma's house,
carrying her hatchet he twirls
in his right hand, half walking,
half skipping; he wonders if
trees think they are part of the earth;
gashing the blade into a midsize maple, stuck,
he tugs, places both feet on the trunk,
falls backward, the blade barely
missing his face, lodges in gray moss.

The forest behind the parsonage
looks old in November, barren-limbed,
the floor coated with crunchy oak leaves,
broken branches, pine cones and needles.
Big Brother is twelve, six feet tall,
rests the twenty-two stock on his shoulder,
locks the sights on a tharn rabbit,
so gray it appears blue in the gloaming,
before it falls, a red bead of blood
where the bullet tore its black nose.

He follows the moonlit railroad tracks
out beyond town, skipping a tie,
toeing a rail, imagining animal eyes
in sinister bushes, thinking a poem
without knowing it yet,
driven by violent sleeplessness,
the silence of the night-neutered dorm.
In his shirt pocket, he carries a letter
his father wrote from his church study,
fear balancing optimism on rails of light.

He stops his trail bike next to a secluded pond,
surrounded by pine trees, the bank
coated with slick needles; stripped
to shorts, he wades muddy water,
chest high, cool clay squishing
between toes. Stroking circles outward
with sunburned arms, he churns
the depths with white farmer's feet,

then laying his face sideways flat
in dark tree shadow he drifts.

There's one mirror in the house,
gaudy gold framed, over the mantle.
Its uneven surface distorts the boy's face.
He watches himself think about baseball,
hammering an apple with a hoe handle,
pretending to be Hank Greenberg.
Dominating the other blue wall, a portrait
of the grandfather he never knew,
a music teacher, looking soft in suit
and tie, who died at 33 "like Jesus."

Big Brother watches the trucks roll
into Tinker, a munitions caravan,
canvas-wrapped, from secret
mountain locations; day after day
his crew of Airmen fork the cargo
from flatbed to transport hold;
a strapping kid from Texas vomits,
unable to believe the mines are unarmed.
Big Brother imagines the splendid green waters
of Tonkin waiting for these heavy seeds.

He thinks there is nothing lonelier
than a motorcycle leaving in the night,
guttural, blue, angrier than a train.
Four AM, the night audit finished, the motel silent,
he wrestles the heavy notion of sleep,

the blinding caffeine headache,
wipes dirt and ink off the green linoleum counter,
walks out front of the lobby where
darkness and fog fuse, thinks of wife and sons
asleep six miles away in this unnatural hour.

The blonde boy hides inside himself
in the space under the steps
of the wading pool. The neighbor
across the street is working on a car.
The boy sits very still, noiseless,
while his brother, returning with
a bathtub boat dances through the crunchy grass,
singing "Born in the USA."
No camera remembers how his frantic mother
found him thirty minutes later hushed as a stone

Here is what he sees sometimes:
negro laborers in the fields,
hoe blades raised to shield
their eyes from the eclipse;
two water fountains at Sears,
one sweet fat black female
elevator attendant; Big Brother
with dead Grandpa's twenty-two
headed for the woods; mean boys
arguing over a stolen bicycle.

The blonde boy grown, hair dulled
to brown, clasped in back to
pony tail between the shoulders

of his cross country captain shirt,
bearded and cool, lover of Louis
Armstrong, Sinatra, Springsteen,
Stipe, Skynyrd, sits cross table at
famous barbecue with country music
singer pictures on the wall, not amused
by the "hippie punk" patron glares.

PLACE

I

You wait for a face
that is a piece of black
broken from the night.

You memorize the coin path
with your fingers:
quarters, dimes, nickels.

Nothing is old or sad,
or pure; car lights, then
ink slides back over.

Heart dragging moon,
the criminal spell
of loneliness.

You wait for a face
long enough in a place like this;
it will come.

II

What did he see when he
came out here past the town
after the dust settled on the war?
Did he tour the landfill ground,
thinking of a restaurant, a motor court
like the ones he'd seen in Asheville?

He'd made his money in monuments
like Wolfe's Gant, powerful hands,
a careful chisel; in walking somewhere,
his nephew had described how he
would go faster and faster till he arrived
at a run, even in his seventies.

When the highway widened
and the town marched slowly
toward his motel, restaurant,
his drive-in theater, it was whispered
that he might be a genius, and soon
folks began to name their sons after him.

III

Once there was a three story motel building
with balconies that overlooked a drive-in screen.

The brick building was flanked by stone veneer
towers and a glass backed racquetball arena.

The rooms were wastefully huge, furnished
more in the style of a rich man's home,

or rather as if a man that had recently
acquired wealth had tapped his wand over them.

Weeknights, the parking lot packed with
canary yellow Mercedes, red Jeep Cherokees.

Long, hot summer weekends, the desk clerks
rented to locals and prayed for their shift to end

before the shit broke loose, for the agnostic moon
to shoot like a cannon ball across the narcotic sky,

for the sex and the whisky to be enough for once,
for the curse of the valley to slither instead

across a competitor's driveway, no OD's,
no acid-fueled balcony leaps,

just the sweet hog-tied depravity that tires
of its game and sleeps like purple mercy.

IV

In the old days,
they sprayed poison
around the buildings
so strong, it killed a snake
that crawled across it.

In the old days,
they designated a good night
at the restaurant when the line
reached across the parking lot
to the red ceramic bull.

In the old days,
they'd leave a fourteen-year-old boy
in charge of the motel
when they took an afternoon off
to drink some shine.

In the old days,
they hired a young Indian
to pick up the condoms
from the gravel humps
at the drive-in theater.

REGISTRY

V

Poovey was holed up for Christmas
in a sixteen dollar/night room,
drove the night auditor crazy
declaring that Frank Borman
would land a plane on 70
to take him home to Long View.

J Bell looked like a retired wino
wearing the same brown suit
every day, would stop for help
tying his tie, show us the same
card trick he could never get right—
stayed with us every other month
till his check ran out and his daughter
came from Jamestown to retrieve him.

Cranford had invented a furniture spring,
claimed to be a retired admiral,
did two hundred pushups every morning,
kept ten dogs in his Chicago apartment,
paid his wife to stay in Key Biscayne,
wore a red bandanna around his neck
and delivered a bone crushing handshake.

Sachs came down from Windsor
to set up security for a gear company;
he was big, tough, ham-fisted,
cold looking as a death camp guard,
claimed his wife was crazy,
he fell in love with one of our housekeepers.
He had a face like a hatchet.

Arlo ran the restaurant;
he looked a little like Floyd the barber,
was a ladies' man, always drove
a white caddy, kept a flower
in his lapel, built a pout house
out behind his lavish mock Tudor;
sometimes he stopped out front
of the lobby like he couldn't
remember where to go.

When the car hit Poovey on
Christmas Eve, he was walking
west on 70 to get coffee at the Lowe's,
a last minute shopper in winter fog,
Frank Borman stooping down
to carry him home to the friendly skies.

VI

Bryn was a sweet young man,
spoke German but may have been Swiss.
His company, a grocery cart manufacturer
had transferred him here for six months.

On the morning he was run over
the weather was foggy; one could
barely see the gray cement
of highway seventy.

Always, we would tell Bryn
not to cross that shivering road,
not to walk beside it to
the store that used their carts.

But the Europeans didn't
seem to understand
the intensity of our drivers,
or the burdens they bore.

The company never retrieved Bryn's stuff
from his room; we gave his clothes
to our housekeepers. I used
his boom box at parties for years.

VII

Stan said he played at Notre Dame,
then for the Sox, back up at first,
told us dugout and locker room
tales, about battles at the plate
with Ford and Reynolds, while
I served the regulars high balls
and beer in the Tower Room,
free drinks on Monday afternoons.

Stan was tall, handsome, funny,
a man's man who sounded a bit
like an Irish Boston beat cop,
and we mentioned him when
we talked about the game; it was
important that we knew someone
who'd been there. When I searched the
Baseball Encyclopedia much later,
I found he had been lying
all along, magnificently,
profoundly, beautifully.

VIII

Charlie was a salesman of some kind,
an ACC football referee on the side.
I used to watch him, stocky, middle-aged,
running the field at Groves Stadium
or Wallace Wade on the Jefferson Pilot broadcasts.
He invited me to his room one afternoon
to teach me to drink scotch,
to tell me about running for town council.

Some things I learned:
all the salesmen had girlfriends;
all the salesmen carried pistols;
furniture is a business of whores;
out of sight, out of mind.

JG stayed with us
because his daddy did,
catholic Martinsville Yankee,
a sixty-five-year-old kid—
one day he challenged me
to a fifty yard dash,
and when I beat him,
had to do it two more times.

Some other things I learned:
our pool contained 20,000 gallons
plus guest urine, sweat and rain;
an ice machine is not too big to steal;
a brain hemorrhage
can bleed through your ear,
your pillow, your bed.

IX

Before

they left the window shade cracked
to watch Big Willie Brown
bounce that little blonde hairdresser
in number one nineteen.

The Yellow taxi driver
with bull ring eyes
performed abortions
in one twenty-five.

The hoochie-coochie girls
from the county fair
paid a week ahead
with one dollar bills.

Black women cleaned rooms
they weren't allowed to rent,
cooked the restaurant's reputation,
hidden in the kitchen.

X

Of course there were the Rabb twins
from somewhere in upstate SC
who stayed in 149–50 for two months,
adjoining single rooms at the midpoint
of the long brick building
known as "Bourbon Alley."
They were in town to paint the stores
in the old furniture mall.

One could throw his voice;
the other was a mute,
and we could not tell them apart
because they were inseparable,
and the one who was mute could
lip synch anything the other one said,
and the speaker was so good;
he could stand in front of you

and make his voice come
from outside the lobby. You can
only imagine the jokes we got them to play,
the stories the one that could talk
could tell, their women swapping,
world fooling shenanigans. The
final joke was when they skipped on the
last week's rent. They were worth it.

XI

Renaldo lived a hundred miles east,
owned a small furniture company,
he had played backup for the Colts,
broke his fingers catching Unitas passes,
lived four nights a week in 105.
We had to be careful not to rent
it through from the weekend or let some
loser shack job tear it up because Renaldo
was Italian, West Virginian,
bigger than life bad ass.

Marty and Merle were college boys;
they carried trash and mowed the lawn,
changed the marquee though
neither of them could spell. Marty
was a baseball player; Merle had
once followed the Grateful Dead for a year.
They kept our utility truck torn up and stole food
out of the restaurant. Afraid of Renaldo,
they scattered when they saw his black Chevy.

Myrna had cleaned the same eighteen rooms
six days a week for thirty years—she was
a small black woman who drove fifteen miles
to work and always finished at 1:30
whether ten rooms were dirty or all eighteen.
She was very shy, rarely talked to customers
or the other housekeepers; her youngest son
had been killed in an Atlanta construction accident.
Renaldo left her a five dollar tip every Friday.
One week she just didn't show up anymore.

XII

Maintenance men, pronounced
maintain-ance, came and went,
Buck, who taught me to shoot a bow
out behind his trailer, was the best;
he'd learned his skills in prison:
electrical, carpentry, plumbing,
he knew how to steal a car,
had lamb chop sideburns and
tattoos across his knuckles.

Drake had been in the Navy,
had a neat appearance and
was efficient with work orders,
as it turns out, throwing them away;
he was, of course, a drunk
who clamored after women
at the pool and showed up
in unrented rooms at night.

The best were always
good men between better jobs,
laid off factory supers,
middle-aged handy men hoping
for an easy route toward retirement.
But a cheap old motel
is an unforgiving broken beast.

Gene had already made his money,
owned a country music joint,
a warehouse, a slew of crazy
looking station wagons,

and an old church. He lasted
the longest, studied the pool,
kept it crystal clear, then there
were Rainmaker, Ott, Earl,
the Dead Head. Jeez,
it was only seven years.

XIII

The old men sat in the plush leather lobby chairs
the owner had placed there as objects of décor.

The old men cleaned their fingernails with
their knives and talked about the war,

or they planned a trip to Georgia
to buy a load of Vidalia onions.

In the summer they talked about the Braves;
sometimes they talked about the old Hickory Rebels,

which often led to motel stories, the lore,
and they laughed at the punch lines,

cackled, chortled, snorted till the owner
walked in, pretending not to notice them,

looking from ceiling to floor as if he
had misplaced a vital possession.

The old men sat for an hour each morning,
hashing and rehashing the past: a retired clerk,

an organ builder, an automobile dealer, a juke joint
entrepreneur, a retired English professor

till they died one by one,
sadly, all.

XIV

Thomas Wolfe's brother Fred
sold for a salt company,
liked to talk about his
famous dead brother's
proclivity for accosting
unfamiliar females
he met on the street.

Lefty Driesell came calling
on Chris Washburn, his
son Chuck, an assistant
in tow, a personable sort
whose doom hung
heavily a few years away;
oh, Lenny, ubi sunt?

Artis Gilmore, Tree Rollins,
Chris Washburn, Nate McMillan,
they had their stays. Bones
McKinney brought folks
from out of town and Tom Shores,
God rest him, all his Carolina
round ballers to sell leather.

Denzel Washington
with his Mercedes St. Elsewhere
ABC brigade arrived to hold up
the highway, to marry
a local beauty queen—
Jim Neighbors, Nurse Kelly
from Mash, Johnny U., too.

XV

Chaos,
when you are not war,
revolution, or murder,
you are a Friday night
at a cheap motel.
You are a crack head crouching
beyond the lobby light,
two requests for rollaways,
a complaint about a high
school party in 208.
You are the growling gut
of a missed dinner,
the drunken woman's
smeared makeup,
showing her tan lines,
asking if the cable has Playboy.
You are the gun lights
of every midnight cruiser,
every fatal picked up chick
waiting in the dark swarm
for the revelry.
You are the moon's arc
over the mountain,
love pledged on
Saturday's balcony,
the unbalanced audit's
miscounted money.
You are the distant siren,
the ring,
the knock,
the broken lock.

XVI

Complaint call at three AM:
it was a bit confusing
when I got there
as it could be
when the world was that size
and one woman had another
in a choke hold
pounding her dyed blonde head
against the gravelly parking lot.

When they rolled over,
screaming, cursing, gouging
in what I would recognize later
as a sort of Jerry Springer maneuver,
their blouses ripped open,
white breasts bouncing,
smeared with blood, marked by teeth
and fingernails—as the mercury
flickered, one of them growled.

The woman fought over
posed in black leather neutrality
under the porch eave,
smoking an indifferent cigarette—
she looked like Joan Jett.
A man staggered from the next door room
to tell me he'd called the cops who
always took an hour to get there
but made it in two minutes this night.

XVII

The hooker was a hollow-eyed junkie,
tall, dark-haired with a pot belly.

I spent a hot September afternoon
running her off; she'd disappear

and I'd think she was gone; then
she would emerge from another room

tramping barefoot down the gray sidewalk,
grabbing a handful of ice from the ice machine,

watching for me. When she finally
called her man to come get her,

a guy in a sleeveless jean jacket
roared into the parking lot, revving

his bike outside the lobby, leaning it
violently on the kickstand.

"You the guy that run Ginny off?"
he asked, wiping at greasy strands

of long hair. "You got it," I said,
regretting that I hadn't called the cops.

"Well, I'll be back for you later,"
he snarled as if he'd rehearsed the line

all the way from the trailer park.
He turned and walked back out

to where Ginny already waited
on the back of the bike. His

left arm was missing, but it
didn't seem to matter. They

were a sight for disturbed eyes.
I never saw them again.

The next day Hurricane Hugo
wrecked the whole town.

XVIII

"Once and For All" they billed it,
and the cable folks convinced me
to rent closed circuit boxes,
to place their colorful poster
against my better judgment
in the remodeled motel lobby.

All afternoon, we talked it up;
first a couple painters, then
a construction crew plopped
down the twenty bucks and
carried their boxes back
to our half-assed televisions.

A local boy, his darkly made up
girl hanging lethargically on his arm;
a fabric salesman with single malt breath;
a former minor league catcher
who sold Miracle Ear hearing aids—
I'm sure there were others.

Several we had to go hook up ourselves;
the signal fluctuated, clear, grainy,
mostly imperfect but recognizable.
When the ninety-one seconds were over,
and Tyson stood over Spinks,
a sweat-less Spartan machine,

I told my night clerk that I needed
to go home and left him to tend

to cable boxes, drunken grumbling
from our disenfranchised sports fans:
no money back, no guarantee,
once and for all.

XIX

The woman screamed into the phone,
my boyfriend is trying to kill himself.

When the auditor got to the room, he found
the drunk, rolling around on the bed,

with a belt around his neck, laughing.
The auditor tamped his pipe and relit it

before walking back uphill to the office.
The night was a cruel black; he could

feel the weight of it and the cancer creeping
in his lungs; Christ, he was tired.

His daughter, a nurse from Florida had
called yesterday about a new treatment.

One AM, the motel audit refused to balance;
he was working and reworking the numbers

when the phone rang; my boyfriend gonna
kill hisself for sure this time. The auditor kept a

forty-five in the desk drawer. His son,
a Highway Patrolman in Maryland had

given it to him for Christmas. He stuck
the pistol in his blazer pocket,

tapped his pipe into the ashtray and headed for
room 125; he felt the adrenaline surge,

his weak knees went solid. Another shit Saturday night,
he would solve at least one problem.

XX

Always said they'd pay tomorrow,
that bearded Rainbow vacuum salesman
and his cute little red headed wife;
the beautiful junkie girl and her
stringy haired boy friend, pungent
and stripped to the waist, their
diapered barefoot toddler, dirty-faced,
tow-headed and silent.
They were waiting for a church
to "sponsor" them, for the boss
to stop by with a check,
for a brother to arrive later,
and every time you heard it,
witnessed the hunger,
their flamboyant desperation,
you knew you had to
kick them to the street,
what would happen
if you didn't, the way
the world comes down
to you or me, buddy,
a mean truth to learn.

XXI

He'd picked her up
at a bar called Yesterdays;
she'd gone to that Pleasure Dome
for the hot legs contest.
But she grew anxious waiting
and took a Quaalude instead.

He drove his CJ 5 beyond
the motel lobby into the dark,
and went in to pay for a single.
The clerk checked his license,
saw he was local and
charged him for a double.

When he got back to the Jeep,
she was gone. He tried to
remember her name to call her.
He drove past each long brick
building, looking for her blue
sundress, listening for her heels.

"That bitch left me, man,"
he told the clerk; "I never went
to the room," he added, laying
the key on the linoleum counter.
The clerk returned the money
after he checked the room.

An hour later, the clerk took
a complaint call from a guest.
A "crazy woman" was creating

a disturbance at the pool. When
he dragged her up out of the pool,
he noticed she was pretty.

He threw one of the motel's
cheap white towels over her
and tried to walk her to the lobby.
She had no pocket book.
She couldn't tell him who she was.
He tried to think what to do.

The night was busy, locals
rolling in off 64-70
in a haze of marijuana
and George Dickel.
She wouldn't shut up
or stay out of the way.

By the time the cops got there,
she had wandered back to the pool,
had passed out on the decking.
Through the lobby window he watched
them walk/carry her to their car.
He noticed she had good legs.

The Great American Spirit.

Chevrolet for the trip back home? A
rolet Div-- of General Mo--
Michigan.

CHEVROLET

SWIMMING

MARCH OF DIMES

Linda Savage
17 C. 8th
Edmond
Oklahoma

XXIII

In the summer there was nothing
like a beautiful girl at the pool.

The salesmen entered the lobby,
sleeves rolled, ties loosened,

peering sideways at the gray-decked
scene, sniffing the hot pavement,

the heavy chlorine, squinting at
the bright flashes of sun on water.

Once, for two weeks, a mother
and daughter lay for hours in

candy striped bikinis
on a Budweiser towel—

chestnut haired and gorgeous
at thirty-five; blonde, sassy

and dangerous at sixteen—
said they were waiting for

work on their house.
A maroon Mercedes sedan

was parked at their room each night.
They were a priceless advertisement,

a voluptuous local mystery,
and when they suddenly departed,

the salesmen offered bribes for a number,
a sample of their wares for that phantom address.

XXIV

One winter it snowed
every Wednesday
for six straight weeks,
sending salesmen home,
stranding employees.
The clerks shared a double
and slept in shifts,
drinking beer, playing cards.

The owner sent me out
in his white Suburban
to fetch the maids
at the projects
over behind the hospital.
I'd plow through each
parking lot, window down,
hollering the motel name.

I also picked up Holiday Inn
which they owned as well,
eight to ten cranky
unwilling women a trip
cramped in the four-wheeler,
scared to death of the snow,
poor and desperate enough
to go anyway.

Night, the snow lay thick
at the bottom of the empty pool.
More fell through mercury light,

piling the scraped driveways,
hiding the highway again.
On the cable in our room,
Reagan delivered his fourth
State of the Union Address.

XXV

I wrote a masters thesis
in a motel room, weekend
manager on duty, typewriter nights;
I answered complaints about myself.

Between check ins
I scribbled pieces of poems,
made up stories about guests,
and I was sending stuff out then,
scrounging for stamps,
checking the post office box.

I can't remember how many times
I crawled under a motel building
at 3 AM to change a fuse,
put the wheels back on a rollaway,
fixed a commode, walked through
pitch black, blessed by the moon.

I became the poet laureate
for the post office whores,
the random darling
of a small legion of fools,
the familiar of charming drunks,
a blundering father
in the no man's land
of the eighties.

When I dove into the pool
to clean the spot by the drain,

ten feet down, I felt
the dreamy pressure of the
whole world above me,
sensed that the water didn't
want to be there either.

XXVI

They'd come from the red dirt roads
out behind the drive-in screen
riding K-Mart bikes with wide
handle bars and banana seats,
popping wheelies up the driveway
past the dried-up fountain,
then weave into a single file
of long-haired punk kids,
hiding their bikes behind the
building that formed its brick mouth
into a horizontal C around the pool,
then sneak up the cement steps out
through the breezeway at 114.

Some days
when I knew the owner was gone,
I'd ignore them for an hour,
their crazed dives and wild whoops,
the cutoff jeans and bruised legs.
But then I'd have to do my job,
sneak around the corner, surprise them
with my voice, "What you boys doing here?"
I'd ask as if I'd never seen them before,
and they'd always reply, playing along,
"We're staying in those rooms back there,"
already filing out the pool gate, wet and
headed back to dirt roads, hot trailers,
dangerous alcoholic stepfathers.

XXVII

Saturday afternoon, the pool area
was a spectacular mess
of scary tattooed guys,
half-drunken pregnant
girlfriends in black bikinis,
screaming blue-eyed children with
red kool-aid stained mouths,
stampeding in cutoff shorts
across the marble deck
as Garth Brooks throbbed
from a Sony ghetto blaster.

It was the summer that
Huey Lewis craved a new drug,
and we were caught between
the struggle to fill rooms
and the need to preserve them.
The owner stopped by
in his yellow Mercedes,
phoned me at home to come
clear out the riff raff.
And I drove north seven miles,
tasting bile and chlorine,

the July clouds gathering
into black and gray hammers.
By the time my Ford pickup
hit the driveway, the thunder
claps started, great drops of
rain splatting the pool, a

sudden north wind ripping
at the awning. I eyed the
vacated scene through slashing
windshield wipers as karma
settled across the scorched valley.

65

WHERE THERE'S ACTION!

CLERKS

XXVIII

There is no afterlife,
only this player piano scroll,
or maybe this is the afterlife
without the whispery protections,
a motel lobby with a single porch light,
a round headed man with a fringe of white hair,
penciling figures on an audit sheet,
and every night he will place
the deposit and the finished books
in the vault in the back room
beside the stairs that go nowhere,
sit in the leather lobby chair,
watching a twelve inch TV,
smoking a pipe filled with
cherry flavored tobacco,
waiting for the slap
of the *Charlotte Observer*
on carpet-covered porch,
waiting for the sun's
heavenly pink, mean arrival.

XXIX

Things had not worked out;
he was out of college, married,
working as a desk clerk at
a small town motor lodge.

A local movie company made a deal
to rent thirty of their cheap rooms
for a month, twelve dollars a night,
two actors/actresses/crew to a single.

The actors would stop by to chat
or to complain about the sorry rooms.
They were in their late teens;
it was to be a goofy teen comedy

with enough nudity to sell tickets.
He would tell the girls that
he was going to be a writer
that working at this motel was

a temporary thing. They'd been
brought in from New York
or New Jersey or Charlotte;
for all of them it was their first film.

The lead actress, Heather, confided that
she would not be staying
in dive motels for long, that
she felt good about this flick.

Every day they would go
to some part of town that had
been roped off so they could
shoot some piece of the film,

and a couple of the girls who
had been hired specifically for
this task would shed their clothes,
and the director who was also

the writer and the only one
who knew what was going on
would say the light was wrong.
One day Heather explained

to the clerk that the light had
to be just right, and he agreed
that that was probably so. They
left a week early because the

shooting turned out to be
not so difficult. When the film
came out, the clerk and his wife
went to see it, and declared

that it had some wit about it
and that it was nice to recognize
the little town on the big screen.
Twenty-five years later

the old clerk can remember
little of his brush with celebrity.
Though he did take a break
from working on his eighth book

to Google that long ago movie.
For most of the actors it was
a one gig resume; Heather,
however, went on to play

a wet t-shirt girl
in another teen picture,
then bowed out with
the lead in a Penthouse joint.

XXX

At the Monopoly Motel,
you had to be good;
you had to size the customer
in one glance, fit him to
the proper section of rooms.
It was about money
or dirty fingernails—
the car he drove up in,
where he parked,
the cut of his suit.
Some days you handed
the customer a key
to go look at an old room,
and you knew you'd
screwed up before
he walked out the door,
and you held your breath
till he returned to tell you
the place was a sty,
yet some of the old guys
who'd stayed for twenty years
would ask for the old rooms,
not just for the cheap rates
but out of the same nostalgia
you feel for an old ball player,
a team from your youth.
But it was mostly economic
segregation, no locals
on Atlantic Avenue,
no construction workers

on Boardwalk—no strippers,
no hookers, no rock bands
not even in Baltic,
not over on Mediterranean.

XXXI

As I carried towels
or fetched rollaways
to the rock-towered
new section of the motel,
and looked southwest,
the drive-in screen loomed,
dully-lit by cheap horror,
the half-dressed blonde
hesitating at a haunted door,
cut to the stage business
of the psychopath's twitching face;
beyond the screen, the ravine,
then a gray layer of forest where I'd
spent a Saturday splitting maple logs
with my father-in-law;
above it the sleeping bear shadow
of Baker's Mountain
which had always caused
a lonely twinge in my stomach
when I came back from college,
that called to me like the scattered
spirit of a long ago vision quest.
And as I clerked my way
through those tedious nights
that I would follow a moon
like the one that shivered
in the sky over Baker's.

XXXII

We were movie buffs then;
they seemed important, huge,
darkly escapist, worlds away
from rent houses, complaining
customers, screaming babies;
we argued Pacino or De Niro,
Walken or Hopper, Streep or
Keaton; we rented VCR's,
sat through cheap matinees,
watched illegal cable boxes
and thought we could maybe
walk out the lobby door
across the reel of moonlight
into Peter Built high beams
projecting our existential future
against the still, black sky.

XXXIII

We thought we'd never grow old;
we thought we'd never get robbed.
There was nothing to do
but fill the place up,
count the money,
and sit back.

One hundred percent occupancy,
so little in the rearview,
no reason to fear tomorrow,
no cause to coax skulls
and machine pistols
from the dark.

And yet we worried the worry
you don't talk about;
the bad news
under the skin,
a movie you can't
look away from,

each of us, silently
searching for an escape,
young enough
to believe
in success
and the cavalry.

XXXIV

Nights off we drove to PB Scotts
to see the Nighthawks to hear
Bob Wenner declare that
"The dance floor is now open,"
to the Double Door to watch
Tinsley Ellis duck walk down
the bar, playing slide with a
long neck Bud, or to UNC-A
to hear Hooker croon "Blues Before
Sunrise," Taj Mahal and Dixon
scorching Spirit Square.
We were blues aficionados,
and the motel was the blues: happy,
sad, red-faced, negro, hillbilly,
men of earth, cauldron-stirring women,
infidels, double-crossers, bill-skippers,
archetypes and psychopaths.
Nights off we spent at Ten Years After
where Bobby Bland wailed and
Sheila Carlisle kicked her skirt high,
where Kenny Greenberg steered White Wolf
was too good for Hickory
and even the bouncers danced.
Back at the motel
everybody thought
we were just clerks.

XXXV

When we took the money to the bank,
we couldn't tell where it came from:
that creased twenty Kennedy laid
on the counter as he cocked his head
and drawled, "I'd like to git a ro-o-o-m;"
three rolls of quarters from that gal who
locked her kids in the room with
cheese crackers and Pepsi while her
boyfriend bought her a restaurant steak;
the company check from the construction
boss at the new waste treatment plant
who told us about picking up two girls
in Waynesville who lived in a cave;
a hundred dollar bill from a coke dealer
fabric salesman with the ace of clubs
accidentally glued to the back of it;
when we made the deposit at the bank,
we didn't care where the money
came from, and the lady at the bank
cared even less.

XXXVI

There's that space between 4:30
and 6:30 AM, the audit balanced,
after hash under glass,
an unnatural time when
ghosts and gravity tangle
outside every lobby window,
and you are too tired to think
how your life is a failed experiment,
about your wasted diploma,
children that would go without
if not for grandparents,
the major that could have
drawn you up from this well.
Nausea, hunger, thirst, fear:
walk through this fractured valley;
wait for the pink tinted east,
unable to read this book
of Carver short stories,
to conceive an easement
from the coming crash.
When the first shift clerk arrives,
you are frantic, your head hammering,
and you will never get used to it
you think as you punch your time card wildly.

XXXVII

Night Auditor—
it's a job. You're lucky
at this age, after the drink,
the divorce, the desperation
of the Reagan economy.
So you show up six nights
a week, shirt and tie,
your ubiquitous pipe tamped,
meticulously work the books,
track mistakes through
imagined transactions,
try not to think about
your first wife with that
buyer in New York City,
grandkids you barely know,
rarely see, the career
that went in the whisky.
It's enough, dealing
with the rabble, the drunks,
the pushy complainers,
the idiot day clerks,
the fools that count
the restaurant take,
solitary hours when
you will not think about
your med school rejection,
cut day for the
college baseball team,
what you had to do
on that ship in the war.

It's a solid job,
and even if
the cancer is creeping,
you wake up sober;
and you go.

XXXVIII

The sound of cats fighting
by the restaurant dumpster defies
the mechanism of description,
the vowels that ooze from the moon
and settle over the stuttering diesel,
the neurotic complaint for its driver,
while the pool pump vibrates under 109,
and the clerk's pacing shoes silently
pad the lobby carpet, worrying
the audit, knowing only faceless names,
room numbers, credit cards,
sleepy wakeup calls, a nimble audience
of vampires cloaked in blackness,
the aimless glory of the lord.

XXXIX

I got a head start on getting behind
in the motel business; poor, sleepy,
living in Dad's river green rental house,
what else was there to do
with my worthless English degree,
poems I wrote in an unheated back room,
first to drive back the lazy decade,
then for publication, either way, worthless.

They spelled congratulations wrong
on the motel marquee when Aaron was born,
red-headed, ready to march to his own
faraway beat, and I cut and carried
the wood to keep him warm, 3 AM,
it all seemed like one of those dreams,
skinny things eating fat things, gods
in the orange eyes of burning coals.

They spelled it right for Thomas Dylan,
four lean years later, a modest house,
where pictures tell a pretty story of sorts,
learning to hit a ball, to ride a bike,
to plant a garden, to keep a dog,
and always that rally between checks,
waiting on wealthy salesmen by day,
reading Tolkien or London to the kids at night.

XL

Like my dad, I survived on
five gallon ideas, that my
children might rise above
where I'd sunk them, nights,
renting the same rooms
over and over, watching
the reel of my past play
across the brain pan of my coma,
two Long Island Iced Teas
at the Steak and Ale Bar
to brave the black snake drive
to fed up wife. I sometime
turned thirty like a pig
rolling over in the red mud,
renting the rundown rooms
again and again, stories
with faces, an emergency room
doc, a university prof come
to study jug face pottery,
a casket dealer who told
this joke about business
going into the hole, drug addicts,
pharmaceutical salesmen,
shack jobs of every persuasion,
and during a lull, a little
gummy hash under the glass,
leaving the oil burnt on the pin,
sending poems out to
the *Paris Review*, the *Carolina
Quarterly*, five gallon ideas

about trailer parks, blues bars,
believed in rescue, fame,
religious mythology,
a bulging symbolism,
that my kids would reach
the Major Leagues.

69

PLAYBOY,
232 East Ohio Street
Chicago, Illinois 60631

THE OLD
CLERK

NO
RIGHT
TURN

STOP

AIRPLANE

Coca-Cola

EAT-RITE DINER

EAT-RITE

XLI

The old clerk was
too much story for one book,
too many old friends stopping by
to punch line his tales.
The old clerk was
the arching eyebrows
of rising action,
the whistling nasal voice
and warm laugh even with
his uncle who built the place, gone;
the restaurant manager, gone;
his best friend, the organ builder,
gone; the great football coach, gone.

When we bore him
from funeral home to hearse,
the old clerk was almost the last,
except for the retired car dealer;
and as they closed the hearse door,
I turned and saw him,
once a big powerful man, leaning
against the pickup truck that hauled
them all to Georgia or Bluefield,
to the farm or to the hardware.
He was the loneliest man
I had ever seen.

XLII

The old clerk tried not to think
of his brother, of his uncle,
of diabetes or heart attacks,
of when his wife,
suspecting him of infidelity,
peppered the window sills.

Yet when he came in
from summer evenings
on the porch to watch the Braves,
he felt the tug of the grave,
and heard the dark report
of his wife's bronchial cough.

No beer, no smokes,
only a grandson to follow
around the yard, the small garden
or the Indian boys from the rentals
next door to wash his car, every day
the sun sinking harder, sooner.

XLIII

The old clerk and the auditor
rode shotgun side in the Suburban—
headed for the ballgame in Atlanta,
Butch at the wheel, me behind him,
his youngest boy and mine in back.

Using the old clerk's hang tag,
we snagged a handicap park
up against the stadium; still the walk,
as many were that weekend, was a
protracted saunter up ramp, down stairs.

The green expanse of field, pitted
between blue seats, gaped in gaudy
magnificence, the boys' first time;
when we found our seats, field level,
the old clerk said, I can't see from here.

The Braves were contenders,
the beginning of their big run;
we had suffered here many times.
The old clerk laughed, joked with
the people around us. The auditor

coughed and wheezed and puffed
on his pipe; he lied about playing
second base. The boys kept their gloves
ready and prayed for foul balls.
Butch and I drank beer and ate peanuts

and promised each other that one day
we'd do better than motel work. On the
way back, the old clerk and the auditor
discussed Hank Williams songs.
Another year, they'd both be dead.

XLIV

He'd had a couple drinks with his lunch,
the day before the fall furniture market,
and though he was chunky and bald,
he had a spring in his step, loud as
any carpetbagger the old clerk
could remember, stopping by the lobby
for no apparent reason, "I've never
seen so many good lookin' whoas
as yous got around here," he bubbled.
"Theys are everywhere," he added.
The old clerk looked down at his feet
like a child embarrassed by praise
till the effect had fully registered
and then, in a melodic voice,
heartbreakingly sincere, he replied,
"We used to have a shit pot full:
every shape, shade or persuasion
till all these Yankees came down here,
married them, and took 'em back home."

XLV

When Japanese businessmen began
to stay at the motel, the old clerk
refused to wait on them, said he'd
fought them thirty-five years ago,
Manila, Guam, a company cook,
said his ugly drunken luck
got him through; his business sense
helped with the locals whose grainy
diets produced loafs of shit in alleys.
The old clerk said "don't trust them
when fiber optic guys toured
their camera-bearing visitors
who became in a miserable year
their biggest competitors.
The old clerk said, I tried to tell you,
and he thought of the *Arizona*,
the timber rattlers in Oregon
where he trained, the son he
didn't see till he was five,
the wounds that vodka and bourbon
could never mend, the tarnished man.

XLVI

While you may have had
a mammy, a maid, a man
who taught the boys
how to shoot squirrels,
the races split,
knew their places,
shopped opposite sides
of the tracks,
though they heard
the lonely complaint
of the same train whistle,
shared a moon, clouds,
great drops of rain,
and you could be
a prince in that world
in a place like Edisto
or later digging in to
the town trenches.
Long after the war had
cracked the wall,
you rented to the first black,
the Gilmore boy from the
Baptist junior college,
said you did it
for Coach Holbrook
as a favor,
but it was clear
you'd sensed
something more.

XLVII

The old clerk had started with his uncle
when he built the motel on the highway
far from the city and its businesses.

When he came back from the war,
his uncle had asked him what he wanted
to do; the times were wide open,

even here in the rural south, the possibilities
endless; he had tried a complaint-ridden
dry cleaning business, a city hotdog stand.

He had run the concession stand
at a drive-in theater, all the while drinking,
telling stories, watching the town move,

first the bowling alley, then the technical college,
car lots, a shopping center, then another,
finally, a mall, announcing the death of the downtown.

Now he watched the fierce metal blades shove
dirt everywhere, and he cursed the strip stores,
yet marveled at the sudden dramatic bloom

that kept the motel full nearly every night.
The old clerk talked about depression summers
on Edisto with his brother, uncle and father,

the strange musical language that was now
like a childhood dream, the truck farming
venture that started all this action.

The old clerk thought of seeds, of black backs bent to the rhythm of heat, of long sandy rows and how everything grows from what's all but forgotten.

XLVIII

Memory is the horseshoe
that sometimes misses the stake,
a smoke ring that drifts
into the foggy morning sky,
and so when I think of the old clerk,
it is not of his worn face
or of his gentle strolling gait,
not of the way he rocked on his heels
when he laughed at his own jokes.
Sixteen years, the face fades,
a man's smell is forgotten,
the spell he cast
on a room of strangers.
I think of the old clerk now,
the shadow he cast over a newspaper,
reading the stock quotes
with a magnifying glass,
the light he moved through
to answer the switchboard,
the million checkouts,
the casual return of change—
the "y'all come back now."

THE Palms MOTOR HOTEL

Free TV

AFTERMATH

66

XLIX

I've still got a dial phone from Mel's Motel
and when it rings, I speak to ghosts:
shacked up doctors and fabric salesmen,
Treasury agents and construction workers,
locals that snuck into the pool,
furniture market hookers, conventioneers,
cab drivers, utterers, junkies—
they tell me why they bet on the Dodgers,
how they listened to Amos n Andy
when they were kids—
and they tell me
about hunting rabbits for food
or watching the old Rebels in the day.
But mostly they want to know about now,
what happened, how we all did
because they are trapped
in a substance called time
and all I've really got is this dial phone
marked with housekeeping, wakeup
service, racquetball, Operator.

L

Grass grows over
where the rows used to be,
where salesmen who
still wore hats stayed,
who drank their bourbon,
wrote up their logs
and called their wives
to make weekend plans.

Rooms that got older
and smaller with
each layer of white latex,
sidewalks painted pale blue,
where a mill owner named Davenport
brought his secretary
every Friday afternoon
for twenty-three years.

Three brick structures,
raised in baseball days,
solid as your grandfather's house.
When I pass through that
rabid intersection by the
haunted vacant yard,
I wonder if I am the only one
who still remembers.

LI

I Say it Like a Prayer

Some mornings I drive by the motel
where I worked for seven years, and
scenes come back to me in flashes:
summertime, a young black man
in shorts and t-shirt stands
outside a room door for hours,
a lead pipe held over his head,
a near-death sentence for his
cheating girlfriend and her honey.
They never come out. He's got
the wrong motel.

A local good ole boy rents a room,
gets stoned while he waits for
his sweetheart to get off from work,
to drop her kid at her mother's.
A knock on his door, a hooker,
and a blow job later, he grins
and laughs, refusing to pay. In a half hour
the bikers that kick his door in
bust the table lamp on his head,
slam him into the TV, piss on him
and leave.

A man calls me one night
to complain about people talking
in the room next door. The rooms
next to him are unrented. Don't
you hear all that? he shouts

when I get to his room. I listen
carefully to nothing, to silence.
You've got to do something about it;
you've got to stop them; it's your job.
I walk next door, knock, turn the lock
and stare into the dark empty room.
You people shut the hell up I holler
angrily. I mean it damn it
I add for good measure. Thanks,
thanks the man tells me as I walk back by him.

Thanks, thanks I say to the motel
as I drive by to my boring safe job
which is rarely anything to write about.
Thanks I say to the ghosts that rise
with lead pipes and biker boots;
thanks I say to the vices and voices.
I say it like a prayer.

About the Author

A past winner of the
Jim Harrison Award,
Tim Peeler has also been a
finalist for the Casey Award
(Baseball Book of the Year).
He lives with his wife,
Penny, in Hickory, North
Carolina, where he directs
the Learning Assistance
Program at Catawba Valley
Community College.
This is his ninth book.

The Hub City Writers Project is a non-profit organization whose mission is to foster a sense of community through the literary arts. We do this by publishing books from and about our community; encouraging, mentoring, and advancing the careers of local writers; and seeking to make Spartanburg a center for the literary arts.

Our metaphor of organization purposefully looks backward to the nineteenth century when Spartanburg was known as the "hub city," a place where railroads converged and departed. At the beginning of the twenty-first century, Spartanburg has become a literary hub of South Carolina with an active and nationally celebrated core group of poets, fiction writers, and essayists. We celebrate these writers—and the ones not yet discovered—as one of our community's greatest assets. William R. Ferris, former director of the Center for Southern Studies, says of the emerging South, "Our culture is our greatest resource. We can shape an economic base…And it won't be an investment that will disappear."

Hub City Anthology • John Lane & Betsy Wakefield Teter, editors

Hub City Music Makers • Peter Cooper

Hub City Christmas • John Lane & Betsy Wakefield Teter, editors

New Southern Harmonies • Rosa Shand, Scott Gould, Deno Trakas, George Singleton

The Best of Radio Free Bubba • Meg Barnhouse, Pate Jobe, Kim Taylor, Gary Phillips

Family Trees: The Peach Culture of the Piedmont • Mike Corbin

Seeing Spartanburg: A History in Images • Philip Racine

The Seasons of Harold Hatcher • Mike Hembree

The Lawson's Fork: Headwaters to Confluence • David Taylor, Gary Henderson

Hub City Anthology 2 • Betsy Wakefield Teter, editor

Inheritance • Janette Turner Hospital, editor

In Morgan's Shadow • A Hub City Murder Mystery

Eureka Mill • Ron Rash

The Place I Live • The Children of Spartanburg County

Textile Town • The Hub City Writers Project

Come to the Cow Pens! • Christine Swager

(continued)

Noticing Eden • Majory Heath Wentworth

Noble Trees of the South Carolina Upstate • Mark Dennis, Michael Dirr, John Lane, Mark Olencki

Literary South Carolina • Edwin Epps

Magical Places • Marion Peter Holt

When the Soldiers Came to Town • Susan Turpin, Carolyn Creal, Ron Crawley, James Crocker

Twenty: South Carolina Poetry Fellows • Kwame Dawes, editor

The Return of Radio Free Bubba • Meg Barnhouse, Pate Jobe, Kim Taylor

Hidden Voices • Kristofer Neely, editor

Wofford: Shining with Untarnished Honor, 1854-2004 • Doyle Boggs, JoAnn Mitchell Brasington, Phillip Stone

South of Main • Beatrice Hill, Brenda Lee, compilers

Cottonwood Trail • Thomas Webster, G.R. Davis, Jr., Peter L. Schmunk

Comfort & Joy: Nine Stories for Christmas • Kirk Neely, June Neely Kern

Courageous Kate: A Daughter of the American Revolution • Sheila Ingle

Common Ties • Katherine Davis Cann

Spartanburg Revisited • Carroll Foster, Mark Olencki, Emily L. Smith

This Threshold: Writing on the End of Life • Scott Neely, editor

Still Home: The Essential Poetry of Spartanburg • Rachel Harkai, editor

The Best of Kudzu Telegraph • John Lane

Stars Fell on Spartanburg • Jeremy L.C. Jones & Betsy Wakefield Teter, editors

Ask Mr. Smartypants • Lane Filler

Two South Carolina Plays • Jon Tuttle

Through the Pale Door • Brian Ray

A Good Mule Is Hard to Find • Kirk H. Neely

For Here or To Go? • Brandy Lindsey & Baker Maultsby, photography by Carroll Foster & Jeffrey Young

Expecting Goodness: The Essential Fiction of Spartanburg • C. Michael Curtis, editor